D1629481

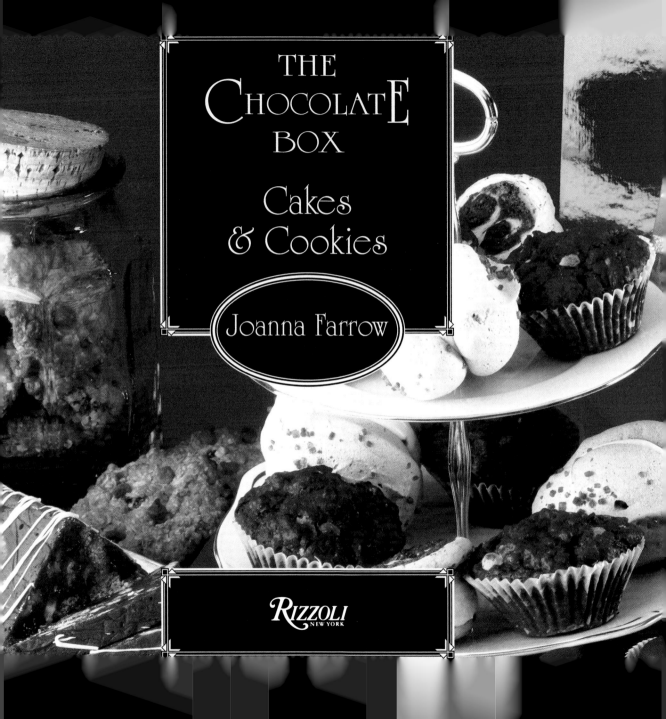

# THE CHOCOLATE BOX

## Cakes & Cookies

Joanna Farrow

*RIZZOLI*
NEW YORK

First published in the United States of America in 1995 by
RIZZOLI INTERNATIONAL PUBLICATIONS, INC.
300 Park Avenue South, New York, NY 10010

First published in the United Kingdom in 1994 by
HARLAXTON PUBLISHING LIMITED
A Member of the Weldon International Group of Companies

Copyright © 1994 : Harlaxton Publishing Limited
Design copyright © 1994 : Harlaxton Publishing Limited

Library of Congress Cataloguing-in-Publication Data
Farrow, Joanna
Chocolate Box/Joanna Farrow
p.   cm.
Includes indexes.
Contents: [1] Cakes & Cookies - - [2] Confectionery & Desserts.
ISBN : 0-8478-1869-1 (set) .
1. Cookery (Chocolate)  2. Desserts.  I. Title.
TX767.C5F39  1995
641.6'374 - - dc20            94-43379 CIP

Publisher:  Robin Burgess
Publishing Manager & Design:  Rachel Rush
Editor:  Alison Leach
Illustrator:  Lyne Breeze, Linden Artists
Photographer:  James Duncan
Home Economist:  Sue Maggs
Stylist:  Madelaine Brehaut
Typesetter:  John Macauley, Seller's
Color separation:  GA Graphics
Printer:  Imago , Singapore

# CONTENTS

Dark, delicious and irresistibly indulgent, chocolate is greeted with more enthusiasm than any other food. Its inimitable texture, which melts, blends, models, and molds, gives it a unique versatility, whether you are serving chocolate chip cookies or an elaborate gâteau.

Supermarkets and confectioners stock a wide range of different chocolates, so it is worth knowing a little about the processing of chocolate before making your choice.

Chocolate is taken from the cacao pod, harvested from the cacao tree which thrives mainly in Africa, Brazil, and Malaysia. After harvesting, the pods are split to reveal cocoa beans. These are sun-fermented for several days to develop their chocolatey flavor. After shelling and roasting, the beans are pressed to produce cocoa solids. The chocolate we buy contains varying quantities of these solids, usually with added sugar and milk. Generally, the higher the percentage of cocoa solids contained in chocolate, the better the flavor and, hence, suitability for special cakes and desserts.

*Opposite: Types of chocolate.*

## Types of Chocolate

### Semisweet Chocolate

This is the richest type of chocolate you can buy, containing about 70% solids. It is generally preferred by chocolate connoisseurs who find other types of chocolate too sweet. Semisweet chocolate can be used instead of dark in cooking when you want a really rich flavor.

### Dark Chocolate

This contains varying amounts of sugar and cocoa solids (anywhere between about 30% and 60%). In the supermarkets it is either stocked in the candy aisle, or with other types of cooking chocolate.

### Milk Chocolate

This contains less cocoa solids (usually around 20%) and has a lot of sugar and milk added. Not surprisingly, when melted and blended with other ingredients, the chocolate flavor and color become rather diluted. Like dark chocolate, it is either stocked in the candy aisle, where you might find one with a higher quantity of cocoa solids, or with other types of cooking chocolate.

### White Chocolate

This contains cocoa butter (extracted during processing) rather than cocoa solids. Large quantities of sugar and milk are added to produce its sweet, creamy flavor. White chocolate will not set as solidly as dark and has a greater tendency to burn.

### Chocolate-Flavored Cake Covering

This is the cheapest form of chocolate and has the least chocolatey flavor. It is made from sugar, vegetable oil, cocoa, and flavoring and has a fatty, bland flavor.

Although inferior in quality, a little added to dark or milk chocolate when melting makes it more stable and easier to shape into curls and other decorations.

### Cocoa Powder

This is made when much of the naturally occurring cocoa butter is removed from the chocolate after roasting. It is usually used to replace some of the flour in chocolate cakes. Drinking chocolate is a mixture of cocoa, sugar, and sometimes dried milk powder. It is unsuitable for cooking but can be used to dust over cakes and desserts.

## Melting Chocolate

There are two easy ways to melt chocolate: in a bowl over hot water or in a microwave.

### Saucepan Method

Break the chocolate into even-sized pieces and place in a heatproof bowl. Rest the bowl over a pan of gently simmering water and leave until melted. The bowl should fit snugly into the pan but must not touch the water level or the chocolate will become overheated.

Once the bowl is removed, make sure no condensation drips into the chocolate or it will seize into a solid mass. Chocolate should only be melted directly in a pan when other liquids are added.

## Microwave Method

Break the chocolate into even-sized pieces and place in a microwave-proof bowl. Microwave on Medium setting allowing 2 minutes for 2 oz/2 squares chocolate and 3 minutes for 8 oz/8 squares chocolate. When butter or syrup is melted with the chocolate, it will take less time. Leave to stand briefly after melting, then stir gently.

## Decorative Ideas

A scattering of grated chocolate or chocolate curls can add the finishing touch to any chocolate cake or gâteau. Once made, the curls will keep in a cool, dry place for a couple of weeks.

## Simple Chocolate Curls

Use a large bar of dark, milk, or white chocolate at room temperature, and pare with a swivel-handled potato peeler. If the chocolate is too cold, it will break into brittle splinters however, it can be microwaved briefly before trying again.

## Chocolate Caraque

Melt about 6 oz/6 squares plain, milk, or white chocolate and spread thinly on a marble slab, smooth work surface or large baking sheet. Leave until set but not brittle. Draw a knife, held at an angle of 45°, across the chocolate to remove small curls. Alternatively, push a clean wallpaper scraper across the chocolate to remove larger curls. If the chocolate breaks into brittle pieces, it is probably too cold and should be left at room temperature before trying again.

## Modeling Chocolate

This is a pliable paste which can be modeled into decorative shapes for decorating cakes and gâteaux, see the Easter Celebration Gâteau (p.64). Fun to use, it can also be made into novelty decorations such as teddy bears and flowers. It will keep in the refrigerator for up to 2 weeks.

Melt 4 oz/4 squares dark, milk, or white chocolate. Beat in 2 tablespoons liquid glucose or light corn syrup until a paste is formed which comes away from the sides of the bowl. Place in a thick plastic bag and leave until firm and pliable. Shape small pieces in the palms of your hands or roll thinly on a work surface lightly dusted with confectioners' sugar.

Gooey, mouthwatering chocolate cakes are, for many of us, what cooking with chocolate is all about. A generous slice of Rich Chocolate Fudge Cake (p.17), dripping with thick cream is the ultimate, thoroughly wicked treat. Just as exciting is the Chocolate-cased Fruit Gâteau (p.20), oozing chocolate cream, or a freshly baked Chocolate Mousse Cake (p.15), the most moist cake imaginable – a must for those who have not tasted this treat before.

Teabreads provide a quick and easy variation on the cake theme. Simple to prepare, their irresistible aroma when cooling makes them impossible to resist, rather like freshly baked bread.

*Previous page: Chocolate Cake with Brandied Figs and Swiss Roll with Chocolate Cream.*

## Chocolate Cake with Brandied Figs

| Serves 12 | 8 oz/1 cup soft margarine |
| | 8 oz/1 cup superfine sugar |
| | 4 eggs |
| | 7 oz/1¾ cups self-raising flour |
| | 1 oz/¼ cup cocoa powder |
| | 2 teaspoons baking powder |
| | 1 tablespoon milk |

| Filling: | 4 oz/1 cup dried figs |
| | ½ teaspoon cornstarch |
| | 3 tablespoons brandy |
| | ¼ pint/⅔ cup plain cultured yoghurt |

| Icing: | 7 oz/7 squares dark chocolate |
| | ½ pint/1¼ cups heavy cream |

| To Decorate: | Chocolate caraque (p.7) |
| | Confectioners' sugar for dusting |

Grease and line two 8 inch layer pans. Place the margarine, sugar, and eggs in a bowl. Sift the flour, cocoa powder, and baking powder into the bowl and beat with an electric beater until creamy and paler in color. Beat in the milk.

Divide the mixture between the prepared pans and level the surfaces. Bake in a preheated oven at 325°F for 25–30 minutes until well risen and just firm to the touch. Transfer to a wire rack to cool.

To make the filling, chop the figs and place in a saucepan with ¼ pint/⅔ cup water. Bring to the boil, reduce the heat and simmer gently for 5 minutes. Blend the cornstarch with a little water and add to the pan. Cook, stirring continuously, until thickened. Remove from the heat and stir in the brandy. Leave to cool.

Place one cake on a serving plate and spread with the yoghurt. Spoon over the fig mixture and cover with the second cake. To make the icing, break the chocolate into pieces. Heat the cream in a saucepan, then stir in the chocolate until it has melted. Leave to cool slightly, then beat the icing and swirl over the top and sides of the cake.

Scatter the chocolate caraque over the cake and serve dusted with confectioners' sugar.

## Variation
Substitute dried prunes, apricots, or dates for the figs.

### Swiss Roll with Chocolate Cream

Serves 8

3 eggs
3 oz/⅓ cup superfine sugar
½ teaspoon ground cinnamon
2½ oz/generous ½ cup all-purpose flour
2 tablespoons cocoa powder

Filling:

¼ pint/⅔ cup heavy cream
2 teaspoons confectioners' sugar
3 oz/¾ cup dark or milk chocolate chips
Confectioners' sugar for dusting

Grease and line a 13x9 inch jelly roll pan with greased non-stick baking parchment.

Place the eggs, sugar, and cinnamon in a heatproof bowl over a saucepan of simmering water. Beat with an electric beater until the mixture leaves a trail when the beater is lifted from the bowl. Remove from the heat and continue beating until cooled. Sift together the flour and cocoa powder, and fold into the mixture carefully, using a large metal spoon.

Spoon into the prepared pan and ease the mixture gently into the corners. Bake in a preheated oven at 400°F for about 15 minutes until just firm to the touch. Place a sheet of parchment paper on a work surface and sprinkle with superfine sugar. Invert the cake on the paper and peel away the lining paper. Starting from a short side, roll up the cake with the paper and leave to cool.

To make the filling, whip the cream with the confectioners' sugar until it is just peaking. Stir in the chocolate chips. Unroll the cake carefully and spread with the cream mixture. Roll up again and transfer to a serving plate. Serve dusted with confectioners' sugar.

## Chocolate Ripple Teabread

Serves 12

7 oz/7 squares dark chocolate
2 oz/2 squares dark or milk chocolate to decorate
7 oz/scant 1 cup unsalted butter or margarine
6 oz/¾ cup superfine sugar
3 eggs
7 oz/1¾ cups self-raising flour
½ teaspoon baking powder
2 teaspoons milk

Lightly grease the base and long sides of a 2 lb loaf pan. Break the dark chocolate into pieces and melt in a heat-proof bowl with 1oz/2 tablespoons of butter or margarine over a saucepan of simmering water.

Place the remaining butter or margarine in a bowl with the sugar, eggs, flour, and baking powder. Beat until light and fluffy; then beat in the milk.

Spoon a quarter of the cake mixture into the prepared pan and level the surface. Spread with a third of the chocolate mixture. Spread with another quarter of the cake mixture and another third of the chocolate. Repeat layering, finishing with a layer of the cake mixture.

Chop the chocolate into small pieces and scatter down the center of the mixture. Bake in a preheated oven at 350°F for about 1 hour until risen and a skewer inserted into the center comes out clean. Leave in the pan for 10 minutes before transferring to a wire rack to cool completely.

*Right: Left to right, Chocolate Ripple Teabread and Spicy Fruit Teabread.*

## Spicy Fruit Teabread

Serves 12-14

10 oz/2 cups mixed dried fruit
6 oz/1 cup light brown sugar
½ pint/1¼ cups cold tea
8 oz/2 cups self-raising flour
1oz/¼ cup cocoa powder
1 teaspoon ground mixed (apple pie) spice
½ teaspoon baking soda
1 egg
1½oz/3 tablespoons candied ginger, finely chopped
2 tablespoons sunflower seeds

Grease and line the base and long sides of a 2 lb loaf pan. Place the mixed dried fruit in a saucepan with the sugar and tea, and bring to the boil. Remove from the heat and leave to cool completely.

Sift the flour, cocoa powder, mixed spice, and baking soda into a bowl. Add the egg, dried fruit mixture, and ginger, and beat until the ingredients are evenly combined.

Spoon into the prepared pan and level the surface. Sprinkle with the sunflower seeds and bake in a preheated oven at 350°F for 1¼–1½ hours until a skewer inserted into the center comes out clean. Leave to cool in the pan for 10 minutes before transferring to a wire rack to cool.

## Chocolate Spiced Parkin

Serves 16

1½ oz/3 tablespoons candied ginger
8 oz/⅔ cup black treacle (molasses)
8 oz/⅔ cup light corn syrup
4 oz/½ cup unsalted butter or margarine
½ teaspoon baking soda
½ pint/1¼ cups milk
1 egg
12 oz/3 cups all-purpose flour
4 oz/1 cup cocoa powder
2 teaspoons ground ginger
12 oz/scant 2½ cups medium oatmeal
2 oz/¼ cup superfine sugar
Extra oatmeal for dusting

Grease and line a 9 inch square cake pan. Slice the ginger as thinly as possible.

Place the treacle, syrup, and butter or margarine in a saucepan and heat gently until the fat has melted. Mix together the baking soda, milk, and egg. Sift the flour and cocoa powder into a bowl. Stir in the oatmeal, sugar and two-thirds of the sliced ginger. Add the molasses mixture and stir until the ingredients are evenly combined. Spoon into the prepared pan and scatter with the reserved candied ginger. Bake in a preheated oven at 350°F for about 45 minutes until just firm to touch. Dust with extra oatmeal and leave to cool in the pan.

### Cook's Tip
Parkin is best eaten 2–3 days after cooking. When cooled, transfer the cake to an airtight container.

*Opposite: Chocolate Spiced Parkin.*

## Chocolate Mousse Cake

Serves 6-8

8 oz/8 squares dark chocolate
4 oz/½ cup unsalted butter
2 tablespoons Cointreau or orange-flavored liqueur
Grated rind of 1 lemon
5 eggs, separated
4 oz/½ cup superfine sugar
Confectioners' sugar for dusting

Grease and line a 9 inch spring form or loose-based round cake pan. Break the chocolate into pieces and place in a heatproof bowl with the butter. Rest over a pan of simmering water and leave until melted. Remove from the heat and stir in the liqueur and lemon rind.

Beat the egg yolks in a bowl with 2 oz/¼ cup of the sugar until it is pale and creamy. Stir in the melted chocolate mixture.

Beat the egg whites in a separate bowl until stiff. Beat in the remaining sugar gradually. Using a large metal spoon, fold a quarter of the whites into the chocolate mixture. Fold in the remainder carefully. Spoon into the prepared pan and bake in a preheated oven at 325°F for about 30 minutes until well risen and the center feels very spongy when pressed gently. Leave to cool in the pan before transferring to a serving plate. Serve dusted with confectioners' sugar.

### Cook's Tip
Because of its high egg content, this cake rises like a soufflé during cooking and deflates gradually when removed from the oven. This produces a delicious cracked crust.

## Chocolate Nut Genoise with Orange Frosting

Serves 10

2 oz/½ cup brazil nuts
1 oz/2 tablespoons unsalted butter
4 eggs
4 oz/½ cup superfine sugar
3 oz/¾ cup all-purpose flour
1 oz/¼ cup cocoa powder
Grated chocolate to decorate

Frosting:

12 oz/1½ cups cream cheese, softened
2 tablespoons confectioners' sugar
Grated rind of 1 orange
4-5 teaspoons orange juice

Grease and line three 7 inch round layer pans. Toast the nuts lightly and chop them. Melt the butter.

Place the eggs and sugar in a heatproof bowl over a saucepan of simmering water and beat until the mixture leaves a trail when the beater is lifted from the bowl. Remove from the heat and beat until the mixture has cooled completely.

Sift the flour and cocoa powder together. Fold half into the egg mixture, then add the butter and nuts and fold in with the remaining flour. Divide the mixture between the prepared pans and bake in a preheated oven at 375°F for 20–25 minutes until risen and just beginning to shrink from the sides of the pan. Transfer to a wire rack to cool.

To make the frosting, beat the soft cheese in a bowl with the confectioners' sugar and orange rind. Add enough orange juice to give a softly peaking consistency.

Place one cake on a serving plate and spread with a third of the frosting. Cover with another cake and spread with another third of the frosting. Finally, add the remaining cake and spread with the remaining frosting. Scatter with grated chocolate and keep in a cool place until ready to serve.

## Chocolate Layer Cake

Serves 10-12

Cake

4 oz/4 squares milk chocolate
8 oz/1 cup soft margarine
8 oz/1 cup superfine sugar
4 eggs
7 oz/1¾ cups self-raising flour
1 oz/¼ cup cocoa powder
2 teaspoons baking powder
1 tablespoon milk

To Decorate:

¼ pint/⅔ cup heavy cream
2 teaspoons confectioners' sugar
Extra confectioners' sugar for dusting

Grease and line two 8 inch layer pans. Chop the chocolate roughly.

Place the margarine, sugar, and eggs in a bowl. Sift the flour, cocoa powder, and baking powder into the bowl, and beat with an electric beater until creamy and paler in color. Beat in the milk and chopped chocolate.

Divide the mixture between the prepared pans and level the surfaces. Bake in a preheated oven at 325°F for 25–30 minutes until well risen and just firm to touch. Transfer to a wire rack to cool.

To decorate the cake, beat the cream lightly with the confectioners' sugar and use this to sandwich the cakes together. Serve dusted with confectioners' sugar.

## Variation
Mascarpone, a very mild, creamy low-fat cheese can be substituted for the cream in the filling. If liked, stir in some chopped walnuts or hazelnuts.

### Rich Chocolate Fudge Cake

Serves 16

8 oz/1 cup soft margarine
12 oz/2 cups light brown sugar
4 eggs
12 oz/2 cups all-purpose flour
1 tablespoon baking powder
4 tablespoons light corn syrup
4 oz/1 cup cocoa powder
¼ pint/⅔ cup soured cream
¼ pint/⅔ cup heavy cream
1 tablespoon confectioners' sugar

Icing:

10 oz/10 squares dark chocolate
2 oz/¼ cup unsalted butter
4 tablespoons milk
8 oz/1⅓ cups confectioners' sugar

To Decorate:

Chocolate caraque (p.7)
Confectioners' sugar for dusting

Grease and line an 8 inch round cake pan. Beat the margarine and sugar together until light and fluffy. Beat the eggs before beating into the creamed mixture gradually, adding a little of the flour to prevent the mixture from curdling. Sift the flour and baking powder

into a separate bowl.

Mix together the corn syrup, cocoa powder, and 6 floz/¾ cup warm water. Stir into the creamed mixture.

Fold half the sifted flour into the mixture; then fold in the sour cream and remaining flour. Spoon into the prepared pan and level the surface. Bake in a preheated oven at 300°F for about 1¼–1½ hours until well risen and a skewer inserted into the center, comes out clean. Leave in the pan for 10 minutes before transferring to a wire rack to cool completely.

Whip the cream with the confectioners' sugar. Split the cake in half and sandwich together with the cream. Place on a serving plate.

To make the icing, break the chocolate into pieces and place in a saucepan with the butter and milk. Heat gently until the chocolate has melted, stirring continuously. Beat in the confectioners' sugar.

Let the icing cool slightly before swirling it over the top and sides of the cake. Scatter the top of the cake with chocolate caraque and serve individual portions dusted with confectioners' sugar.

## Cook's Tip
The chocolate caraque is not essential but it does make the cake look even more irresistible. Coarsely grated chocolate can be used as an easier alternative.

*Next page: Left to right, Chocolate Nut Genoise with Orange Frosting and Chocolate Layer Cake.*

## Chocolate-Cased Fruit Gâteau

Serves 10-12

4 eggs
4 oz/⅔ cup light brown sugar
4 oz/1 cup all-purpose flour
2 oz/2 squares white chocolate, finely grated
6 oz /6 squares dark chocolate

Filling:
1 lb mixed soft fruit, such as strawberries,
raspberries, cherries, redcurrants, and blackcurrants
2 tablespoons superfine sugar
4 tablespoons Kirsch
¼ pint/2 cups heavy cream

Grease and line a 7 inch round cake pan. Place the eggs and sugar in a heatproof bowl over a saucepan of simmering water and beat until the mixture leaves a trail when the beater is lifted from the bowl. Remove from the heat and beat the mixture until it has cooled. Sift the flour over the mixture. Add the grated chocolate and fold in using a large metal spoon. Spoon into the prepared pan and bake in a preheated oven at 350°F for about 30 minutes until just firm to the touch. Transfer to a wire rack to cool completely.

To make the filling, mix the soft fruit in a bowl and add the sugar and Kirsch. Toss very gently. Whip the cream. Split the cake horizontally and place one half on a serving plate. Spread with a little of the cream and cover with half the fruit, reserving any excess juices that are left in the fruit bowl. Cover with the second half of the cake. Stir any juices into the remaining cream and swirl it over the top and sides of the cake.

Break the dark chocolate into pieces and melt in a heatproof bowl over a saucepan of simmering water. Measure the circumference of the cake, using a piece of string. Cut a piece of baking parchment, 1 inch longer than the circumference and 1 inch deeper than the cake. Spread the melted chocolate over the paper, taking it to within ½ inch of the ends and in a wavy line about ½ inch from one long side. Spread chocolate almost to the edge of the remaining long side. Leave the chocolate until it is no longer runny, then carefully position it around the cake with the long straight edge around the base of the cake and the ends just touching down the side. Chill until the chocolate has set and then peel away the paper carefully. Just before serving, scatter the top of the cake with the reserved soft fruit.

### Cook's Tip
The chocolate collar is surprisingly easy to position as long as you do so when the chocolate is no longer runny, but not yet beginning to set. If necessary, get someone to help to support the collar while you wrap it around the cake.

*Opposite: Chocolate-Cased Fruit Gâteau*

## Devils Food Cake

4 oz/4 squares dark chocolate
8 fl oz/1 cup milk
8 oz/2 cups all-purpose flour
½ teaspoon baking soda
2 teaspoons baking powder
2 tablespoons cocoa powder
5 oz/⅔ cup soft margarine
10 oz/1⅔ cups light brown sugar
3 eggs

Filling:
¼ pint/⅔ cup heavy cream
3 tablespoons dark brown sugar

Frosting:
1 egg white
6 oz/¾ cup superfine sugar
Pinch of cream of tartar

Grease and line the base and sides of an 7 inch round cake pan. Break the chocolate into pieces and place in a saucepan with the milk. Heat gently, stirring continuously until it has melted. Leave to cool.

Sift together the flour, baking soda, baking powder, and cocoa powder. Beat the margarine and sugar together until light and fluffy. Beat in the eggs gradually, adding a little of the flour to prevent the mixture from curdling. Fold in half the flour mixture, then the chocolate mixture. Fold in the remaining flour.

Spoon the mixture into the pan and bake in a preheated oven at 350°F for about 45 minutes until risen and a skewer inserted into the center, comes out clean. Leave to cool in the pan.

To make the filling, whip the cream lightly. Cut the cake horizontally into three layers. Place one layer on a serving plate and spread with half the cream. Sprinkle with half the sugar. Cover with a second layer and cover with the remaining cream and sugar. Cover with the remaining layer.

To make the frosting, place all the ingredients in a heatproof bowl with 2 tablespoons hot water. Rest over a saucepan of simmering water and beat with an electric beater until the frosting stands in soft peaks. Spread the frosting immediately over the top and sides of the cake.

## White Chocolate and Banana Teabread

Serves 12
5 oz/5 squares white chocolate,
plus 1½oz/1½ squares white chocolate to decorate
3 small bananas
9 oz/2¼ cups self-raising flour
1 teaspoon baking powder
4½oz/generous ½cup unsalted butter or margarine
4½oz/generous ½cup superfine sugar
Grated rind of 1 lemon
3 eggs

Grease and line the base and long sides of a 2 lb loaf pan. Chop the chocolate into small pieces. Peel and mash the bananas.

Sift the flour and baking powder into a bowl. Cut the butter or margarine into small pieces and rub into the flour with your fingertips. Add the sugar, lemon rind, eggs, banana, and chocolate, and beat until the ingredients are evenly combined.

Spoon into the prepared pan and level the surface. Bake

in a preheated oven at 350°F for about 50–60 minutes until well risen and a skewer inserted into the center comes out clean. Leave in the pan for 10 minutes before transferring to a wire rack to cool completely.

To decorate the teabread, break the chocolate into pieces and melt in a heatproof bowl over a saucepan of simmering water. Using a teaspoon, drizzle the melted chocolate over the teabread and swirl lightly with the tip of a toothpick. Leave to set.

## Variation
Substitute dark or milk chocolate for the white and replace 1 oz/¼ cup of the self-raising flour with cocoa powder. Add a little ground mixed (apple pie) spice if liked.

## Chocolate Cookie Pyramid

Serves 10-12

10 oz graham crackers
or shortbread cookies
18 oz/18 squares dark chocolate
12 fl oz/1½ cups evaporated milk
6 oz/1½ cups mixed nuts, such as almonds,
hazelnuts, peanuts, and walnuts, roughly chopped
4 oz/⅔ cup raisins
2 oz/2 squares dark or white chocolate to decorate

Line the base and three sides of a 4 x 8 inch loaf pan with plastic wrap. Chop the cookies into chunks.

Break the chocolate into pieces and place in a saucepan with the evaporated milk. Heat gently, stirring continuously until the chocolate has melted. Remove from the heat and transfer to a bowl. Leave to cool.

Stir the nuts into the chocolate mixture with the raisins and cookies Prop the prepared pan on a carton so that the base of the pan is tilted to an angle of 45° and the unlined side of the pan is uppermost. Spoon the cake mixture into the pan and level the surface. Leave to set.

Remove the cake carefully from the pan and peel away the plastic wrap. Place on a serving plate. To decorate the cake, break the chocolate into pieces and melt in a heatproof bowl over a saucepan of simmering water. Place in a pastry tube fitted with a writing tip and use to pipe decorative lines over the cake.

Keep in a cool place until ready to serve.

## Cook's Tip
When the cake has hardened sufficiently, the pan can be transferred to the refrigerator to speed up setting. Remove from the refrigerator for about 30 minutes before serving to make slicing easier.

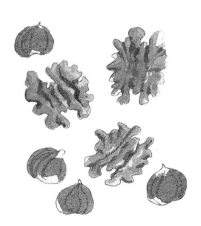

Crumbly biscuits and cookies, lavishly spread or speckled with melting chunks of chocolate, are fun to make and irresistibly addictive to eat. This chapter includes a variety of shapes, sizes, and textures, from huge American-style cookies to delicate wafer tuiles that make the perfect accompaniment to coffee, or to provide texture with a creamy chocolate pudding.

Home-made cookies do not generally have the keeping qualities of bought cookies, so avoid making too many at once. If a recipe makes more than required, refrigerate half the uncooked mixture and make up a fresh batch a day or so later. This applies in particular to gingerbread cookies, macaroons, and those made with oatmeal.

*Previous page: Left to right, Double Chocolate Creams, White Chocolate Fingers, and Cocoa Spice Cookies.*

## White Chocolate Fingers

Makes about 12    2 oz/½ cup slivered almonds
2 oz/2 squares white chocolate
2 oz/¼ cup unsalted butter or margarine, softened
1½ oz/3 tablespoons superfine sugar
Grated rind of 1 lemon
2 oz/½ cup all-purpose flour
1 oz/¼ cup ground almonds
Confectioners' sugar for dusting

Grease a large baking sheet lightly. Break the slivered almonds roughly into smaller pieces. Chop the chocolate into small pieces.

Cream the butter or margarine and sugar together until light and fluffy. Stir in the lemon rind, flour, ground almonds, and chopped chocolate to make a firm paste. Knead the mixture lightly, then roll out a quarter of it on a lightly floured work surface to a sausage, about ½ inch in diameter. Cut into 2 inch lengths. Roll in the slivered almonds until lightly coated; then transfer to the prepared baking sheet. Repeat with the remaining mixture.

Bake the cookies in a preheated oven at 325°F for about 8 minutes until turning golden. Leave on the baking sheet for 3 minutes before transferring to a wire rack to cool completely. Dust generously with confectioners' sugar.

## Variation
Use chopped dark, milk, or orange flavored chocolate instead of the white. For a darker coloring replace 2 tablespoons of the flour with cocoa powder and dust with cocoa powder after baking.

## Cocoa Spice Cookies

Makes 24

4 oz/½ cup unsalted butter
or margarine, softened
4 oz/⅔ cup light brown sugar
1 egg yolk
7 oz/1¾ cups all-purpose flour
1 oz/¼ cup cocoa powder
1 teaspoon ground mixed (apple pie) spice
2 oz/⅓ cup sultanas (golden raisins)
1 oz/3 tablespoons currants
Milk to mix
Superfine sugar to sprinkle

Grease two baking sheets lightly. Cream together the butter or margarine and sugar until light and fluffy. Stir in the egg yolk. Sift the flour, cocoa powder, and mixed spice into the bowl. Add the sultanas and currants, and mix to a firm dough, adding a little milk if the mixture is dry. Knead the dough lightly and roll out on a floured work surface. Cut out 2 inch rounds, using a cookie cutter. Transfer the cookies to the prepared baking sheets and sprinkle with superfine sugar. Bake in a preheated oven at 350°F for 15–20 minutes until slightly darker. Leave on the baking sheets for 3 minutes before transferring to a wire rack to cool completely.

## Double Chocolate Creams

Makes 15

5½ oz/scant 1½ cups all-purpose flour
2 tablespoons cocoa powder
4 oz/½ cup unsalted butter
2 oz/¼ cup superfine sugar

To Finish:

2 oz/2 squares white chocolate
Cocoa powder for dusting

Grease a large baking sheet lightly. Sift the flour and cocoa powder into a bowl. Cut the butter into small pieces and rub into the flour with your fingertips. Stir in the sugar and knead until the mixture makes a firm dough. (Alternatively, mix the ingredients to a dough in a food processor.)

Roll out the dough on a lightly floured work surface to a 10½x7½ inch rectangle. Transfer to the baking sheet and mark a 10x7 inch rectangle. Mark the rectangle lengthways into three strips, then across the strips at 1 inch intervals to make 30 rectangles. Prick with a fork and bake in a preheated oven at 400°F for 15 minutes. Remove from the oven and cut through the marked lines while still warm, discarding the excess cookie around the edges. Transfer the cookies to a wire rack to cool.

To finish the cookies, break the white chocolate into pieces and melt in a heatproof bowl over a saucepan of simmering water. Use the white chocolate to sandwich the cookies together in pairs. Leave to set; then dust lightly with cocoa powder.

## Chocolate Florentines

Makes about 30

4 oz/¾ cup slivered almonds
1 oz/2 tablespoons glacé (candied) cherries
1½ oz/3 tablespoons unsalted butter
4 tablespoons heavy cream
2 oz/¼ cup superfine sugar
1 oz/2 tablespoons chopped mixed peel
½ oz/2 tablespoons all-purpose flour

To Decorate:

3 oz/3 squares dark chocolate
3 oz/3 squares white chocolate

Line two baking sheets with non-stick baking parchment. Crumble the almonds roughly into smaller flakes. Chop the glacé cherries into smaller pieces. Melt the butter in a small saucepan with the cream and sugar. Bring to the boil and remove from the heat. Stir in the almonds, cherries, mixed peel, and flour. Beat together until evenly mixed.

Place teaspoonfuls of the mixture, spaced well apart, on the prepared baking sheets. Bake in a preheated oven at 350°F for 6–8 minutes until the mixture has spread and is turning golden around·the edges. Use a lightly oiled round cookie cutter to bring the edges of each cookie towards the center, creating neat round shapes. Transfer to a wire rack to cool. Bake any remaining mixture in the same way.

Break the dark chocolate into pieces and melt in a heatproof bowl over a saucepan of simmering water. Melt the white chocolate in the same way and keep separate. Spread the dark chocolate over the back of half the cookies and the white chocolate over the remaining cookies. Finish by marking wavy lines with a fork. Return to the wire rack until set.

## Brandy Snap Cigars

Makes 10–12

2 oz/¼ cup unsalted butter
3 oz/¼ cup light corn syrup
1½ oz/3 tablespoons superfine sugar
2 tablespoons cocoa powder
2 oz/½ cup all-purpose flour
2 oz/2 squares dark or milk chocolate to decorate

Line a large baking sheet with non-stick baking parchment. Place the butter, syrup, and sugar in a small saucepan and heat gently until the butter has melted. Remove from the heat. Sift the cocoa powder and flour into the pan and stir well.

Spoon 4 teaspoonfuls of the mixture, spaced well apart, on to the prepared baking sheet and bake in a preheated oven at 375°F for about 5 minutes until the mixture has spread and is just turning a darker color around the edges. Leave to cool for about 30 seconds, then peel a cookie away from the paper and wrap around the handle of a wooden spoon. Remove from the spoon and shape the remaining cookies. Transfer to a wire rack to cool while cooking the remaining mixture in batches.

To decorate the cookies, break the chocolate into pieces and melt in a heatproof bowl over a pan of simmering water. Dip the ends of the cookies in the melted chocolate; then transfer them to a sheet of parchment paper to set.

### Cook's Tip
If the cookies harden before you have shaped them, return them to the oven for a few moments to soften.

*Left: Chocolate Florentines.*

## Chunky Chocolate Chip Cookies

Makes 6

3 oz/3 squares dark chocolate
5 oz/1¼ cups all-purpose flour
½ teaspoon baking soda
2½ oz/scant ½ cup light brown sugar
2 oz/¼ cup unsalted butter or margarine
1 teaspoon vanilla extract
1 tablespoon light corn syrup
1 egg

Grease a large baking sheet lightly. Chop the chocolate into small pieces. Sift the flour and baking soda into a bowl. Stir in the sugar.

Melt the butter or margarine in a small saucepan and add to the bowl with the vanilla extract and corn syrup. Beat the egg and measure 2 tablespoons into the bowl. Beat the ingredients together until blended, then add the chocolate pieces.

Divide the mixture into six portions. Shape each into a cake and place on the prepared baking sheet, flattening each slightly. Bake in a preheated oven at 375°F for 15–20 minutes, until turning darker around the edges. Leave on the baking sheet for 5 minutes before transferring to a wire rack to cool completely.

*Right: Left to right, Chunky Chocolate Chip Cookies and Chewy Chocolate Oat Cookies.*

## Chewy Chocolate Oat Cookies

Makes 16

4 oz/1 cup self-raising flour
½ teaspoon baking soda
5 oz/1½ cups oatmeal
2 oz/⅓ cup prunes
5 oz/⅔ cup unsalted butter or margarine
5 oz/scant 1 cup light brown sugar
1 tablespoon light corn syrup
3 oz/¾ cup dark or milk chocolate chips
Confectioners' sugar or cocoa powder for dusting

Grease two baking sheets lightly. Sift the flour and the baking soda into a bowl. Stir in the oatmeal. Chop the prunes roughly.

Put the butter or margarine, sugar, and corn syrup in a small saucepan and heat gently until the butter is melted. Remove from the heat and add to the flour mixture, stirring until evenly combined.

Leave to cool for 20 minutes, then stir in the chocolate and prunes. Spoon tablespoonfuls of the mixture, spaced well apart, on to the prepared baking sheets. Bake in a preheated oven at 350°F for about 15 minutes until golden. Leave on the baking sheets for 3 minutes before transferring to a wire rack to cool completely. Serve dusted with confectioners' sugar or cocoa powder.

### Variation
Use dried apricots, dates, or figs instead of the prunes.

## Chocolate Coffee Palmiers

Makes 25

1 oz/1 square dark chocolate
2 oz/¼ cup superfine sugar
1 tablespoon instant espresso powder
9 oz puff pastry
Beaten egg to glaze

Grease 2 baking sheets lightly. Grate the chocolate finely and mix in a small bowl with half the sugar and the coffee.

Roll out the pastry on a work surface, sprinkling with the remaining sugar as you roll, to an 11 inch square. Trim off the edges and brush the pastry with a little beaten egg. Sprinkle with the chocolate mixture. Roll up the pastry from one side to the center. Roll up the other side to meet the first roll. Moisten the rolls with beaten egg and press together firmly.

Using a sharp knife, cut the roll into thin slices and transfer the pastry to the prepared baking sheets. Flatten slightly with the back of a fork, then bake in a preheated oven at 425°F for 10–15 minutes until golden. Transfer the cookies to a wire rack to cool.

## Variation

These simple cookies can be transformed into delicious teatime pastries if sandwiched in pairs with cream.

## Chocolate Walnut Crisps

Makes about 30

1½ oz/⅓ cup walnuts
4 oz/½ cup unsalted butter, softened
3 oz/½ cup confectioners' sugar
1 teaspoon vanilla extract
4 oz/1 cup self-raising flour
2 tablespoons cocoa powder
Confectioners' sugar for dusting

Grease two baking sheets lightly. Chop the walnuts fairly finely.

*Above: Chocolate Peanut Shortbread.*

## Chocolate Peanut Shortbread

Makes 10

2 oz/⅓ cup shelled peanuts, roughly chopped
2 oz/2 squares milk chocolate
3 oz/⅜ cup unsalted butter, softened
2 oz/¼ cup crunchy peanut butter
2 oz/¼ cup superfine sugar
6 oz/1½ cups all-purpose flour
Cocoa powder or confectioners' sugar for dusting

Place an 8 inch flan ring on a baking sheet and grease lightly or use an 8 inch loose-base cake pan.

Cream the butter, peanut butter, and sugar together until smooth. Work in the flour gradually to form a dough. Press the mixture into the flan ring or pan and flatten with the back of a spoon. Mark into 10 portions.

Chop the chocolate into small pieces and scatter with the peanuts, pressing them down lightly. Bake in a pre-heated oven at 350°F for 20–25 minutes until the nuts are turning golden. Remove from the oven and cut into 10 wedges along the marked lines. Leave to cool in the pan before serving the wedges dusted with the cocoa powder or confectioners' sugar.

Beat the butter and sugar together until pale and stir in the vanilla extract. Sift the flour and cocoa powder into the bowl and mix to a firm paste. Chill for about 30 minutes.

Place teaspoonfuls of the mixture on the prepared baking sheets. Flatten slightly with the back of a fork; then scatter with the chopped walnuts. Bake in a preheated oven at 350°F for 8–10 minutes until the mixture has spread and the nuts are turning golden. Leave on the baking sheet for 3 minutes, then transfer to a wire rack to cool. Serve dusted with confectioners' sugar.

## Chocolate Ginger Cookies

Makes 15-20
11 oz/2¾ cups all-purpose flour
1 oz/¼ cup cocoa powder
1 teaspoon ground ginger
1 teaspoon ground mixed spice (apple pie spice)
1 teaspoon baking soda
4 oz/½ cup unsalted butter
6 oz/¾ cup superfine sugar
4 teaspoons light corn syrup
1 egg
1 oz/1 square dark chocolate

Grease two baking sheets lightly. Sift the flour, cocoa powder, ginger, mixed spice, and baking soda into a bowl. Cut the butter into small pieces and rub into the flour mixture with your fingertips.

Add the sugar, syrup, and egg, and mix to a firm dough. Knead lightly until smooth. Roll out half the mixture on a lightly floured work surface and cut out shapes, using gingerbread cutters. Transfer them to the prepared baking sheets and bake in a preheated oven at 375°F for about 15 minutes until slightly risen. Leave on the baking sheets for 5 minutes before carefully transferring to a wire rack to cool completely. Roll out the remaining mixture and bake in the same way.

To decorate the cookies, break the chocolate into pieces and melt in a heatproof bowl over a saucepan of simmering water. Using a fine paintbrush, paint decorative features such as buttons and faces on to the cookies. Leave to set.

*Right: Chocolate Ginger Cookies.*

## Variation

If you do not have any gingerbread cutters, use plain or novelty-shaped cookie cutters. After baking, these can also be painted attractively with the melted chocolate.

### Miniature Chocolate Macaroons

Makes about 20

2 oz/½ cup ground almonds
1 oz/1 square dark chocolate
2 oz/¼ cup superfine sugar
½ teaspoon vanilla or almond extract
½ teaspoon cocoa powder
1 egg white
1 oz/¼ cup slivered almonds

Line a large baking sheet with non-stick baking parchment. Toast the ground almonds lightly, watching closely as soon as they start to color. Leave to cool. Break the chocolate into pieces and melt in a heatproof bowl over a saucepan of simmering water.

Mix the ground almonds in a bowl with the sugar, vanilla or almond extract, cocoa powder, and melted chocolate. Whisk the egg white lightly and add to the bowl gradually to make a firm paste.

Place small teaspoonfuls of the mixture on the prepared baking sheet and flatten slightly. Crush the slivered almonds lightly between your fingers, then scatter them over the macaroons. Bake in a preheated oven at 400°F for 8–10 minutes until just firm. Remove the macaroons from the paper and transfer to a wire rack to cool.

These small cakes, generally made in slabs and cut into fingers or squares, are ideal for transporting, making perfect fillers for lunch boxes and picnics. The choice is invitingly varied from sponge-based cakes to flaky fruit bakes and crumbly shortbread slices. If you do not have the correct pan, they will not be spoiled in a similar-sized pan, just keep an eye on the cooking time. When cooled, slice the cake, which will keep for several days in an airtight container.

## Sticky Pear Bake

Makes 16

4 large ripe pears
5 oz/⅔ cup unsalted butter, softened
1 oz/1½ tablespoons light brown sugar
4 oz/½ cup superfine sugar
4 oz/¾ cup self-raising flour
2 tablespoons cocoa powder
½ teaspoon baking powder
2 eggs

Grease and line the base of a 9 inch square shallow baking pan. Peel, quarter, and core the pears. Cut into thick slices.

Melt ½oz/1 tablespoon of the butter in a saucepan. Add the pears and soften in the butter for 3 minutes. Arrange in a single layer in the base of the pan. Put the brown sugar in the pan with 2 tablespoons water. Cook, stirring continuously until the sugar has dissolved; then cook rapidly until very syrupy. Stir in another ½oz/1 tablespoon of the butter until melted then pour the syrup over the pears.

Place the remaining butter in a bowl with the superfine sugar. Sift the flour, cocoa powder, and baking powder into the bowl. Add the eggs and beat well until light and fluffy. Spoon over the pears and level the surface. Bake in a preheated oven at 350°F for about 30 minutes until risen and firm in the center.

Leave in the pan for 5 minutes. Loosen the edges of the cake with a knife, then invert on to a flat plate and peel away the lining paper. Leave to cool slightly and serve cut into squares.

*Opposite: Sticky Pear Bake.*

## Streusel Slices

Makes 14

4 oz/4 squares dark chocolate
9 oz/2¼ cups self-raising flour
1 teaspoon ground mixed (apple pie) spice
Finely grated rind of 1 lemon
6 oz/¾ cup unsalted butter
5 oz/scant 1 cup light brown sugar
2 oz/½ cup ground almonds
1 egg
2 tablespoons cocoa powder
Confectioners' sugar or cocoa powder for dusting

Grease a 14x4½ inch loose-based rectangular flan pan lightly. Chop the chocolate into small pieces. Sift the flour and spice into a bowl. Add the lemon rind and the butter, cut into small pieces. Rub the butter into the flour until the mixture begins to cling together. Add the sugar and almonds and mix until crumbly. Reserve a third of the mixture and beat the egg into the remainder. Mix to a dough consistency.

Press the dough into the prepared pan. Stir the chopped chocolate and cocoa powder into the reserved crumble mixture. Scatter over the base in an even layer. Bake the Streusel in a preheated oven at 350°F for 35–40 minutes until slightly risen and turning golden.

Leave to cool slightly in the pan, then cut into slices and transfer to a wire rack. Serve dusted with confectioners' sugar or cocoa powder.

## Chocolate Espresso Squares

Makes 15

6 oz/¾ cup margarine, softened
6 oz/¾ cup superfine sugar
6 oz/1½ cups self-raising flour
1 oz/¼ cup cocoa powder
1 teaspoon baking powder
4 teaspoons instant espresso powder
3 eggs
1 tablespoon milk
5 oz/1¼ cups walnut pieces

Icing:

4 oz/4 squares dark chocolate
3 tablespoons light corn syrup
1 oz/2 tablespoons unsalted butter

Grease and line a 13x9 inch jelly roll pan. Put the margarine and sugar in a bowl. Sift the flour, cocoa powder, and coffee powder into the bowl. Add the eggs and beat with an electric mixer until light and fluffy. Stir in the milk. Spread the mixture into the prepared pan and level the surface. Scatter with the walnut pieces. Bake in a preheated oven at 325°F for about 25 minutes until risen and just firm to the touch.

To make the icing, break the chocolate into pieces and place in a heavy-based saucepan with the syrup, butter, and 3 tablespoons water. Heat gently, stirring continuously until the chocolate is melted and the mixture is smooth. Spoon over the cake; then cut into squares.

*Opposite: Left to right: Warm Cheesecake Squares and Apple and Chocolate Puffs.*

### Chocolate Pecan Slices

Makes 10

3 oz/¾ cup self-raising flour
2 oz/¼ cup unsalted butter
1 oz/2 tablespoons light brown sugar
4 oz/1 cup pecan nuts

To Finish:

½ teaspoon cornstarch
5 tablespoons orange juice
4 fl oz/½ cup maple syrup
2 oz/2 squares dark chocolate

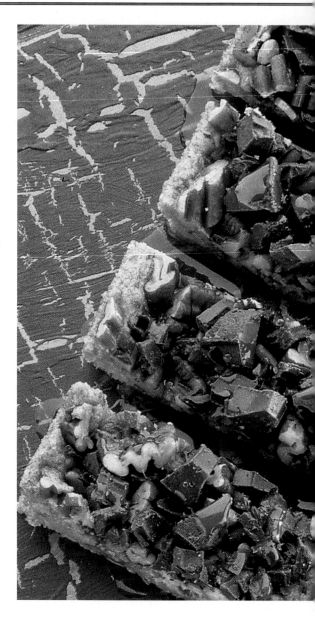

Grease the base and sides of a 6 inch square loose-base cake pan lightly.

Sift the flour into a bowl. Cut the butter into small pieces and rub into the flour with your fingertips. Stir in the sugar and mix to a firm dough. Press into the prepared pan and level with the back of a teaspoon. Chop the pecan nuts very lightly and scatter over the surface. Bake in a preheated oven at 350°F for about 20 minutes until slightly risen and beginning to color around the edges.

Blend the cornstarch with a little of the orange juice in a small saucepan. Blend in the remaining orange juice and the maple syrup. Cook over a moderate heat, stirring continuously, until the mixture is clear and thickened. Leave to cool slightly; then brush the syrup over the pecan base. Leave to cool completely. Remove the sides of the pan. Chop the chocolate and scatter over the cake. Cut the cake into 10 wedges.

### Variation

For a mild coffee flavoring, add 1 teaspoon instant coffee to the flour. If liked, substitute walnuts for the pecans.

## Warm Cheesecake Squares

Makes 16

4 oz graham crackers
2 oz/¼ cup unsalted butter

Cheesecake:

2 oz/½ cup hazelnuts
4 oz/4 squares dark chocolate
8 oz/1 cup cottage cheese
2 eggs
4 oz/½ cup superfine sugar
¼ pint/⅔ cup heavy cream
1 oz/¼ cup cocoa powder
Confectioners' sugar for dusting

Grease the sides of an 8 inch square shallow baking pan. Place the crackers in a thick plastic bag and crush with a rolling pin. Melt the butter in a saucepan. Add the crackers, stirring until evenly coated. Turn into the prepared pan and press down lightly.

To make the cheesecake, chop the nuts roughly and break the chocolate into pieces. Press the cottage cheese through a sieve into a bowl. Separate the eggs and add the yolks to the bowl with the sugar, cream, and cocoa powder. Beat well until smooth; then stir in the nuts and chopped chocolate.

Beat the egg whites until stiff; then fold a quarter into the chocolate mixture, using a large metal spoon. Fold in the remainder carefully. Spoon into the pan and level the surface. Bake in a preheated oven at 325°F for about 1½ hours until just firm. Leave to cool slightly, then cut into squares and serve warm, dusted with confectioners' sugar.

*Left: Chocolate Pecan Slices.*

## Millionaire's Shortbread

Makes 12

3 oz/¾ cup all-purpose flour
2 oz/¼ cup unsalted butter
1 oz/2 tablespoons superfine sugar

Topping:

2 oz/¼ cup unsalted butter
2 oz/¼ cup superfine sugar
14 oz can sweetened condensed milk
5 oz/5 squares dark chocolate

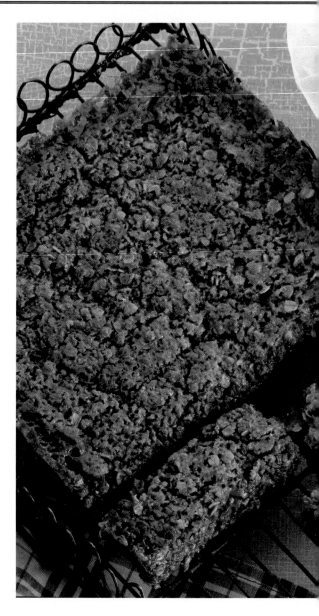

Grease a 7 inch square cake pan lightly. Sift the flour into a bowl. Cut the butter into small pieces and rub into the flour with your fingertips. Add the sugar and mix to a firm dough. Press the mixture into the prepared pan and level with the back of a spoon. Bake in a preheated oven at 350°F for about 20 minutes, or until just beginning to color around the edges. Leave to cool in the pan.

To make the caramel topping, place the butter, sugar, and condensed milk in a heavy-based saucepan. Heat gently, stirring continuously, until the sugar has dissolved. Bring to the boil, then reduce the heat and simmer for about 5 minutes until slightly thickened. Pour over the shortbread base and leave to cool completely.

Break the chocolate into pieces and melt in a heatproof bowl over a saucepan of simmering water. Remove from the heat and stir lightly. Pour the chocolate over the caramel and spread to the edges of the pan. Chill until set. To serve the shortbread, cut into pieces and remove from the pan carefully.

*Right: Sticky Flapjacks.*

## Cook's Tip
Serve the shortbread in small portions. It is delicious but extremely rich!

### Sticky Flapjacks

Makes 20

4 oz/4 squares dark chocolate
6 oz/¾ cup unsalted butter or margarine
4 oz/½ cup superfine sugar
4 oz/¾ cup dark brown sugar
4 oz/⅓ cup light corn syrup
15 oz/4½ cups oatmeal

Grease a 10x7 inch shallow baking pan lightly. Chop the chocolate roughly.

Put the butter or margarine into a heavy-based saucepan with both sugars and the syrup. Cook over a moderate heat until the sugar has melted. Remove from the heat and beat in the oats; then add the chopped chocolate.

Spoon the mixture into the prepared pan, spreading into the corners and levelling with the back of a teaspoon. Bake in a preheated oven at 350°F for about 25 minutes until slightly risen and coloring around the edges. Leave to cool slightly in the pan; then mark into 20 fingers.

## Cook's Tip
If you prefer, pack the mixture into the pan and scatter the chopped chocolate on top.

## Apple and Chocolate Puffs

Makes 10

2 lb cooking apples
1 tablespoon lemon juice
7 oz/7 squares dark chocolate
½ teaspoon ground cinnamon
1 oz/2 tablespoons unsalted butter
1 lb puff pastry
1 oz/2 tablespoons superfine sugar
2 oz/⅓ cup sultanas (golden raisins)
Beaten egg to glaze
Superfine sugar to sprinkle

Grease a 13x9 inch jelly roll pan lightly. Peel, quarter, and core the apples. Cut into fairly thick slices and place in a bowl of cold water with the lemon juice.

Break the chocolate into pieces and put in a heatproof bowl with the cinnamon and butter. Melt over a saucepan of simmering water.

Halve the pastry and roll out one half thinly on a floured work surface to a rectangle slightly larger than the pan. Lay it in the pan, pressing the pastry up the sides. Drain the apples thoroughly and toss them in the sugar. Scatter the apples in an even layer over the pastry. Sprinkle with the sultanas. Stir the chocolate mixture lightly and place small spoonfuls over the apples until partially covered. Brush the edges of the pastry with a little beaten egg.

Roll out the remaining pastry and lay over the filling, pressing the edges of the pastry together firmly to seal. Brush with beaten egg; then mark decorative diagonal lines over the pastry. Sprinkle with sugar and bake in a preheated oven at 425°F for about 25 minutes until risen and golden.

Leave to cool; serve warm or cold, cut into rectangles.

### Variation
Ripe pears make an equally good alternative to the apples. Toss them in half the quantity of superfine sugar to allow for their sweeter flavor.

## White Chocolate Fingers

Makes 16

6 oz ginger snap cookies
3 oz/⅓ cup unsalted butter
4 oz/4 squares white chocolate
1 oz/⅓ cup shredded coconut

Topping:

3 oz /3 squares white chocolate
2 oz/¼ cup unsalted butter or margarine, softened
2 oz/¼ cup superfine sugar
3 oz/¾ cup self-raising flour
1 oz/½ cup shredded coconut
Finely grated rind of 1 lemon
1 teaspoon ground ginger
2 tablespoons milk
3 oz/3 squares white chocolate to decorate

To make the base, place the cookies in a thick plastic bag and crush them with a rolling pin. Melt the butter and mix with the cookies. Spread into the base of a 10x7 inch shallow baking pan. Press the mixture down gently with the back of a spoon.

Break the white chocolate into pieces and melt in a heatproof bowl over a saucepan of simmering water. Stir in the coconut and spread over the base. Chill.

To make the topping, break the white chocolate into pieces and melt as above. Beat the butter or margarine and sugar together until light and fluffy. Add the flour, coconut, lemon rind, ginger, milk, and melted chocolate, and beat until smooth. Spread over the prepared base and bake in a preheated oven at 375°F for about 25 minutes until slightly risen and golden. Leave to cool slightly; then cut into fingers. Transfer to a wire rack to cool completely.

To decorate, melt the white chocolate as above and place in a pastry tube fitted with a writing tip. Use to drizzle lines over the fingers. Leave until set.

Chocolate is a favorite flavoring for many classic teatime cakes and many are included in this chapter. Pretty meringues, tartlets, and éclairs use a subtle chocolate flavoring, while the brownies, muffins, cup cakes, and strudels use chocolate in more robust quantities.

For maximum enjoyment, some of the small cakes should be served warm. The croissants, oozing chocolate sauce and almond paste, make an excellent mid-morning treat, while the Chocolate and Orange Drop Scones (p.51), dripping in orange butter, are perfect as a teatime snack. Likewise, the quick and easy Chocolate Cinnamon Doughnuts (p.54) are delicious eaten freshly fried, although any leftovers will reheat in a moderate oven.

## White Chocolate and Strawberry Tartlets

| | |
|---|---|
| Makes 8 | 6 oz/1½ cups all-purpose flour |
| | 3 oz/⅓ cup unsalted butter |
| | 3 egg yolks |
| | 1 oz/2 tablespoons superfine sugar |
| | |
| Filling: | 4 oz/4 squares white chocolate |
| | 8 fl oz/1 cup heavy cream |
| | |
| To Decorate: | 8 oz/1½ cups strawberries |
| | 4 tablespoons redcurrant jelly |
| | White chocolate caraque (p.7) |

Sift the flour into a bowl. Cut the butter into small pieces, and rub into the flour with your fingertips. Stir in the egg yolks and sugar, and mix to a firm dough, adding a few drops of water if the mixture is too dry. Knead lightly until smooth and chill for 30 minutes.

Roll out the pastry on a lightly floured work surface. Cut into eight portions and use to line eight individual flan pans, about 3½ inches in diameter. Line each pan with baking parchment and fill with baking beans. Bake in a preheated oven at 375°F for 15 minutes until turning golden around the edges. Remove the beans and paper, return to the oven for a further 5 minutes. Leave to cool.

To make the filling, break the chocolate into pieces. Pour half the cream into a saucepan and bring just to the boil. Remove from the heat and stir in the chocolate until it has melted. Spoon the mixture into a bowl and stir in the remaining cream. Leave to cool; then beat until it is just

*Previous page: Left to right, White Chocolate Strawberry Tartlets, Chocolate Whirls (p.50), and Chocolate and Orange Eclairs.*

peaking. Spread the chocolate cream into the tartlet cases.

To decorate the tartlets, cut the strawberries into thin slices and arrange over the filling. Melt the redcurrant jelly in a saucepan with 1 tablespoon water. Leave to cool until beginning to thicken; then use the jelly to glaze the tartlets. Decorate with white chocolate caraque and chill until ready to serve.

## Chocolate and Orange Éclairs

| | |
|---|---|
| Makes about 16 | 2½ oz/½ cup all-purpose flour plus 2 tablespoons all-purpose flour |
| | 2 oz/¼ cup unsalted butter |
| | 2 eggs |
| | |
| Filling: | ¼ pint/⅔ cup heavy cream |
| | Finely grated rind of ½ orange |
| | 1 teaspoon confectioners' sugar |
| | |
| To Decorate: | 6 oz/6 squares dark chocolate |
| | 2 oz/⅓ cup confectioners' sugar |
| | 1 teaspoon orange juice |

Grease two baking sheets lightly and moisten them. Sift the flour into a bowl. Place the butter in a small pan with ¼ pint/⅔ cup water and heat gently until the butter has melted. Bring to the boil, remove from the heat and add the flour immediately. Beat thoroughly with a wooden spoon. Continue beating over the heat until the mixture is smooth and comes away cleanly from the sides of the pan. Leave to cool for 2 minutes.

Beat the eggs and beat into the flour mixture gradually, a little at a time until the mixture is glossy. Place in a pastry bag fitted with a ½ inch plain tip and pipe fingers, about 2½ inches long on to the baking sheets.

Bake in a preheated oven at 400°F for 20–25 minutes until well risen and golden. Reduce the oven temperature to 350°F. Make a slit along the side of each éclair and return to the oven for a further 5 minutes to dry out the centers. Transfer to a wire rack to cool.

To make the filling, beat the cream, orange rind, and confectioners' sugar until it is just peaking. Spoon or pipe the cream into the éclairs.

To decorate the éclairs, break the chocolate into pieces and melt in a heatproof bowl over a saucepan of simmering water. Blend the confectioners' sugar with enough orange juice to give the consistency of pouring cream. Spread a little chocolate over each éclair, then spoon a little of the orange icing over the chocolate. Using the tip of a toothpick, swirl the icing into the chocolate.

## Chocolate Whirls

Makes 12     7 oz/scant 1 cup unsalted butter, softened
2 oz/⅓ cup confectioners' sugar
7 oz/1¾ cups all-purpose flour
1 oz/¼ cup cocoa powder
½ teaspoon baking powder

To Decorate:     3 oz/3 squares dark chocolate
Cocoa powder for dusting

Line a 12-section cupcake pan with paper cases. Beat the butter and confectioners' sugar together until pale and creamy. Sift the flour, cocoa powder, and baking powder into the bowl and beat in to make a smooth, soft paste.

Spoon the mixture into a large pastry tube fitted with a large star tip. Pile swirls into the centers of the cases, leaving a small cavity in the center. Bake in a preheated oven at 375°F for 15–20 minutes until risen; then transfer to a wire rack to cool.

To decorate, break the chocolate into pieces and melt in a heatproof bowl over a saucepan of simmering water. Spoon a little into the center of each whirl. Leave to set; then serve dusted with cocoa powder.

## Cook's Tip
If you do not have a large bag and tip, spoon the mixture into the cases and make a cavity with the back of a teaspoon before baking.

*Right: Chocolate and Orange Drop Scones.*

## Chocolate and Orange Drop Scones

Serves 6

4 oz/4 squares dark or milk chocolate
4 oz/1 cup self-raising flour
½ teaspoon baking powder
2 tablespoons superfine sugar
1 egg
7 fl oz/scant 1 cup milk
Oil for shallow-frying

Orange Butter:  3 oz/⅓ cup unsalted butter, softened
2 tablespoons confectioners' sugar
Finely grated rind of 1 orange

To make the orange butter, place the butter, confectioners' sugar, and the orange rind in a bowl with 1 teaspoon hot water and beat until light and fluffy. Transfer to a small serving dish and chill.

To make the scones, cut the chocolate into small pieces. Sift the flour and baking powder into a bowl and stir in the sugar. Make a well in the center and add the egg and a little of the milk. Beat the mixture to a batter; then beat in the remaining milk and the chocolate pieces.

Heat a little oil in a frying pan or griddle. Add spoonfuls of the batter and fry gently until turning golden on the underside. Flip over the scones and fry again until golden. Drain and keep warm while cooking the remainder.

Serve the drop scones warm, accompanied by the orange butter.

## Chocolate Almond Brownies

Makes 18

6 oz/1½ cups blanched almonds
1 lb dark chocolate
8 oz/1 cup unsalted butter or margarine, softened
3 eggs
8 oz/1⅓ cups light brown sugar
3 oz/¾ cup self-raising flour
1 teaspoon almond extract

Grease and line a 10x7 inch shallow baking pan. Chop the almonds very roughly and lightly toast them. Chop 4 oz/4 squares of the chocolate finely and reserve.

Break the remaining chocolate into pieces and put in a heatproof bowl with the butter or margarine. Melt over a saucepan of simmering water.

Beat together the eggs and sugar in a bowl. Beat in the melted chocolate mixture gradually. Sift the flour over the mixture and fold in with the almonds, almond extract and chopped chocolate.

Spoon the mixture into the prepared pan and bake in a preheated oven at 375°F for about 35 minutes until the surface is crusty and feels only just firm. Leave to cool in the pan, then turn out and cut into portions.

## Cook's Tip
When cooked the cake should be crusty on the surface but feel quite soft underneath. This cools to a deliciously moist, gooey texture.

*Right: Chocolate Almond Brownies.*

## Chocolate Cup Cakes

| Makes 12 | 3 oz/3 squares milk chocolate |
| | 2 oz/¼ cup soft margarine |
| | 2 oz/¼ cup superfine sugar |
| | 1 egg |
| | 1½ oz/⅓ cup self-raising flour |
| | 2 tablespoons cocoa powder |
| | |
| Icing: | 6 oz/6 squares dark chocolate |
| | 3 tablespoons orange juice |
| | 93 oz/½ cup confectioners' sugar |

Line a 12-section cupcake pan with paper cases. Chop the milk chocolate roughly.

Place the margarine, sugar, egg, flour, and cocoa powder in a bowl and beat until smooth and paler in color. Stir in the chopped chocolate. Divide the mixture between the paper cases and bake in a preheated oven at 350°F for about 10 minutes until risen and just firm. Leave to cool.

To make the icing, break the chocolate into pieces and put in a heatproof bowl with the orange juice. Rest the bowl over a saucepan of simmering water and leave until melted. Stir in the confectioners' sugar.

Spread the chocolate cakes with the icing. Leave to set.

## Variation
For two-tone chocolate cup cakes, substitute white chocolate for the dark in the icing.

### Chocolate Cinnamon Doughnuts

Makes 8
4 oz/4 squares dark chocolate
½ oz/1 tablespoon unsalted butter
9½ oz packet bread mix
or equal quantity of prepared sweet bread dough
½ teaspoon ground cinnamon
1 tablespoon superfine sugar

To Finish:
Oil for deep-frying
2 oz/¼ cup superfine sugar
2 teaspoons ground cinnamon

Break the chocolate into pieces and place in a heatproof bowl with the butter. Leave until melted. Place the bread mix and cinnamon in a bowl and make up with milk or water following the packet directions. Knead and leave to rise in a warm place until doubled in size.

Put the dough on a lightly floured work surface and knead lightly. Divide into eight portions. Roll out one piece to a round, about 4 inches in diameter. Place a spoonful of the chocolate mixture in the center. Bring the edges of the dough up around the chocolate and pinch together to enclose it. Place on a lightly greased baking sheet. Shape the remaining doughnuts in the same way. Cover them loosely with oiled plastic wrap and leave to rise again until doubled in size.

Heat the oil in a deep-frying pan until a little dough sizzles on the surface. Add 2–3 doughnuts to the pan and fry for about 3 minutes until puffed and golden. Remove with a slotted spoon and drain on paper towels. Mix the sugar and cinnamon on a plate and use to coat the doughnuts. Serve freshly made.

## Cook's Tip

Avoid letting the oil get too hot, or the doughnuts will be crusty and overbrowned on the surface while still raw in the center.

## Mini Chocolate Strudels

Makes 9

4 oz/4 squares dark chocolate
2 oz/½ cup walnuts
2 oz/⅓ cup raisins
½ teaspoon ground mixed (apple pie) spice
1½ oz/3 tablespoons unsalted butter
3 large sheets filo pastry
Cocoa powder for dusting

Grease a baking sheet lightly. Break the chocolate into pieces and melt in a heatproof bowl over a saucepan of simmering water. Chop the walnuts roughly and mix with the chocolate, raisins, and mixed spice.

Melt the butter. Cut the pastry sheets widthways into three, to give nine rectangles. Brush over each with the melted butter. Spoon the chocolate down the center of each rectangle. Fold the long edges over the filling; then roll up each to make small strudels.

Place with the joins underneath on the baking sheet and brush with the remaining butter. Bake in a preheated oven at 400°F for about 10 minutes until golden. Serve warm or cold, dusted with cocoa powder.

*Left: Chocolate Cinnamon Doughnuts.*

## Double Chocolate Chip Muffins

Makes 12

6 oz/6 squares dark chocolate
12 oz/3 cups self-raising flour
1 tablespoon baking powder
3 oz/¾ cup cocoa powder
3 oz/½ cup light brown sugar
3 oz/¾ cup dark chocolate chips
3 oz/¾ cup white chocolate chips
13 fl oz/1⅝ cups milk
6 tablespoons vegetable oil
2 teaspoons vanilla extract
1 egg
1 egg yolk

Line a 12-section cupcake pan with muffin papers. Break the chocolate into pieces and melt in a heatproof bowl over a saucepan of simmering water.

Sift the flour, baking powder, and cocoa powder into a bowl. Stir in the sugar and chocolate chips. Beat together the milk, oil, vanilla extract, egg, and egg yolk. Add to the bowl with the melted chocolate and fold in gently until the ingredients are just combined.

Spoon the mixture into the paper cases, piling it up in the center. Bake in a preheated oven at 425°F for 20 minutes until well risen and just firm. Transfer to a wire rack to cool completely.

### Cook's Tip

Muffin tins and cases are slightly larger than ordinary tartlet ones. If you do not have any, use the smaller size and bake the mixture in two batches.

## Chocolate Frangipane Croissants

Makes 6

6 small croissants
4 oz/4 squares dark chocolate
1 oz/2 tablespoons unsalted butter
3 oz almond paste
Confectioners' sugar for dusting

Halve each croissant and place the bases on a baking sheet. Break the chocolate into pieces and place in a heatproof bowl with the butter. Rest over a saucepan of simmering water and leave until melted. Cut the almond paste into thin slices.

Arrange the almond paste slices over the croissant bases; then spoon over the chocolate mixture. Replace the croissant tops. Warm in a preheated oven at 350°F for 5–10 minutes and serve dusted with confectioners' sugar.

*Left: Chocolate Frangipane Croissants.*

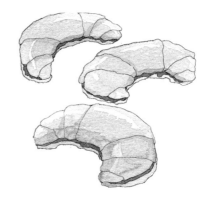

## Chocolate Meringue Pairs

Makes 12-14

4 egg whites
8 oz/1 cup superfine sugar
2 tablespoons cocoa powder
4 tablespoons granulated sugar or turbinado sugar crystals
¼ pint/⅔ cup heavy cream to decorate

Line two baking sheets with non-stick baking parchment. Beat the egg whites until stiff. Beat in half the sugar gradually, a tablespoon at a time. Sift the cocoa powder over the meringue and beat in. Beat in the remaining sugar gradually until the meringue is stiff and glossy.

Place spoonfuls of the meringue, spaced slightly apart, on the prepared baking sheets. Crush the sugar lightly if it is very coarse and sprinkle over the meringues. Bake in a preheated oven at 250°F for 1–1½ hours until the meringues are crisp. Remove from the oven and peel away the paper.

Whip the cream lightly until it is just peaking. Sandwich together pairs of meringues by spooning or piping the cream to secure.

## Variation

Adding some cocoa powder makes these meringues mildly chocolatey. For a richer flavor sandwich the meringues with chocolate ganache. Heat ¼ pint/⅔ cup heavy cream in a pan; then stir in 5 oz/5 squares dark chocolate until melted. When cooled, beat the mixture until it is peaking.

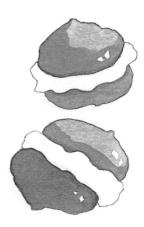

Choose a chocolate cake for a birthday celebration and it will undoubtedly be a winner. In this chapter there is a simple Birthday Parcel Cake (p.62), attractively finished with ribbon ties, or a stunning chocolate box which you can fill with fresh cream truffles or a selection of chocolates. Either cake will delight the recipient, regardless of age.

A classic requirement on the Christmas table is the chocolate log, Buche de Noël (p.70), a light rolled sponge, filled with cream and lavishly spread with chocolate ganache. Sugar-dusted chocolate curls make a simple, but effective, decoration for this mouthwatering centerpiece.

*Next page: Left to right, Chocolate Truffle Box (p.63) and Birthday Parcel Cake (p.63).*

## Birthday Parcel Cake

Serves 20

6 oz/¾ cup soft margarine
6 oz/¾ cup superfine sugar
3 eggs
5½ oz/1¼ cups self-raising flour
2 tablespoons cocoa powder
1 teaspoon baking powder
5 tablespoons Amaretto liqueur or orange-flavored liqueur
4 oz/4 squares dark chocolate
5 tablespoons heavy cream

To Decorate:

3 tablespoons apricot jam
1½ lb white marzipan (almond paste)
6 oz/6 squares semisweet chocolate
2 tablespoons light corn syrup
1 egg white
1 lb confectioners' sugar
Cornstarch for dusting
Ribbons

Grease and line a 10x7 inch shallow baking pan. Place the margarine, sugar, and eggs in a bowl. Sift the flour, cocoa powder, and baking powder into the bowl. Beat well with an electric beater until paler in color and creamy. Turn into the prepared pan and level the surface. Bake in a preheated oven at 325°F for about 35–40 minutes until risen and just firm to the touch. Transfer to a wire rack and leave to cool.

Cut off any excess dome from the center of the cake; then cut widthways into three equal pieces. Drizzle the cakes with the liqueur.

Break the chocolate into pieces and place in a small heavy-based saucepan with the cream. Heat gently until the chocolate has melted; then transfer to a bowl. Leave to cool; then beat until the mixture is just peaking. Spread over two of the cakes and sandwich them together on a serving plate.

Melt the apricot jam and press through a sieve into a small bowl. Brush the jam over the top and sides of the cake. Knead the almond paste lightly and then roll it out and use to cover the top and sides of the cake.

Break the semisweet chocolate into pieces and place in a heatproof bowl with the corn syrup. Place over a saucepan of simmering water and leave until melted. Remove from the heat and cool slightly. Add the egg white and a little of the confectioners' sugar. Beat with an electric mixer until smooth, adding more confectioners' sugar gradually. When too stiff to stir, turn the mixture out on to the work surface and knead in more confectioners' sugar to make a stiff paste. Roll out a quarter on a surface dusted with confectioners' sugar and use to cover the top of the cake. Use the remainder to cover the sides. Using hands dusted with cornstarch, smooth the icing to eliminate creases. Leave in a cool place to harden. Decorate the cake with ribbons to resemble a parcel.

### Cook's Tip

This makes a perfect cake for any chocoholic celebrating a birthday, and can be finished with as many ribbons as you think suitable. The chocolate icing has a slightly softer texture when warm. If left to cool it sets fairly hard but can be softened by kneading or microwaving it briefly.

## Chocolate Truffle Box

Serves 16

1 oz/2 tablespoons unsalted butter
3 eggs
3 oz/⅓ cup superfine sugar
2½ oz/½ cup plus 2 tablespoons all-purpose flour
2 tablespoons cocoa powder

To Decorate:

¾ pint/2 cups heavy cream
1 tablespoon confectioners' sugar
3 tablespoons brandy, rum, or orange-flavored liqueur
7 oz/7 squares dark chocolate
25 bought or home-made chocolate truffles
Paper candy cases
Ribbon (optional)

Grease the base and sides of a 7 inch square cake pan. Melt the butter and reserve. Place the eggs and sugar in a large heatproof bowl over a saucepan of simmering water. Using an electric mixer beat the mixture until it leaves a trail when the beater is lifted.

Remove from the heat and continue beating until cooled. Sift half the flour and cocoa powder over the mixture. Drizzle the melted butter around the edges of the bowl. Using a large metal spoon fold in the flour and butter carefully. Sift over the remaining flour and cocoa powder, and fold in. Turn into the prepared pan and bake in a preheated oven at 350°F for 20–25 minutes until risen and just firm to the touch. Leave to cool.

To decorate the cake, place the cream, sugar, and liqueur in a bowl and beat until it is just peaking. Split the cake in half horizontally and sandwich together with a little of the whipped cream. Spread the top and sides of the cake with the remaining whipped cream.

Break the chocolate into pieces and melt in a heatproof bowl over a saucepan of simmering water. Crumple a sheet of foil lightly and then completely flatten it so that the foil retains some creases. Cut the foil into a 9½x7½ inch rectangle. Spread the melted chocolate over the foil to within ¼ inch of the edges. Leave to set.

When completely set, trim the rectangle to 9x7 inches; then cut widthways into four equal strips. Peel the foil away carefully from the chocolate and position one strip on each side of the cake so that the corners meet. Place the truffles in paper candy cases and arrange on top of the cake. Chill until ready to serve, and decorate, if liked, with a ribbon.

## Easter Celebration Gâteau

Serves 20

8 fl oz/1 cup milk
1 tablespoon white wine vinegar
4 oz/4 squares semisweet chocolate
4 oz/½ cup soft margarine
8 oz/1 cup superfine sugar
2 eggs
11 oz/2¾ cups self-raising flour
1 teaspoon baking powder
2 tablespoons cocoa powder
2 teaspoons ground mixed spice
4 oz/⅔ cup mixed dried fruit

To Decorate:
4 oz/½ cup unsalted butter, softened
8 oz/1½ cups confectioners' sugar
1 oz/¼ cup cocoa powder
Double quantity chocolate modeling paste (p.7)
About 9 oz miniature chocolate eggs
Ribbon (optional)

Grease and line an 7 inch round cake pan. Mix the milk with the vinegar. Break up the chocolate and melt in a heatproof bowl over a saucepan of simmering water.

Put the margarine, sugar, and eggs into a bowl. Sift the flour, baking powder, cocoa powder, and mixed spice into the bowl. Add half the milk and beat until the mixture is smooth and paler in color. Add the remaining milk, the melted chocolate, and dried fruit and mix until evenly combined. Turn into the prepared pan and level the surface. Bake in a preheated oven at 325°F for 1¼–1½ hours until a skewer, inserted into the center, comes out clean. Leave to cool.

To decorate the cake, beat together the butter, confectioners' sugar, and cocoa powder with 2 teaspoons hot water until smooth and creamy. Split the cake in half horizontally and sandwich with a little of the buttercream. Place on a serving plate. Spread the remaining buttercream over the top and sides.

Knead a little of the modeling paste lightly and roll out to a strip, slightly deeper than the cake and about 6 inches long. Gather up the strip slightly and secure loosely to the side of the cake. Make and secure more strips until the sides are completely covered. Pile the chocolate eggs into the center of the cake. Keep the cake in a cool place until needed. If liked, finish the sides of the cake with ribbon.

## Cook's Tip
Chocolate mini eggs often come wrapped in colorful foil. If liked, leave some of the eggs in their wrappers, matching the colors with the decorative ribbon.

*Opposite: Easter Celebration Gâteau.*

## White Chocolate Gâteau

Serves 16

8 oz/1 cup margarine, softened
8 oz/1 cup superfine sugar
Finely grated rind of 1 orange
4 eggs
8 oz/2 cups self-raising flour
1 teaspoon baking powder
1 tablespoon milk
6 tablespoons Cointreau

Filling:

4 oz/¾ cup strawberries
4 oz/¾ cup raspberries
2 teaspoons superfine sugar
¼ pint/⅝ cup heavy cream

To Decorate:

7 oz/7 squares white chocolate
½ pint/1¼ cups heavy cream
White chocolate caraque (p.7)
Cocoa powder or confectioners' sugar for dusting

Grease and line two 8 inch layer cake pans. Place the margarine, sugar, orange rind, and eggs in a bowl. Sift the flour and baking powder into the bowl and beat well until light and fluffy. Beat in the milk. Bake in a pre-heated oven at 325°F for 25–30 minutes until risen and just firm to the touch. Transfer to a wire rack to cool; then drizzle the sponges with the Cointreau.

To make the filling, slice the strawberries roughly and toss in a bowl with the raspberries and sugar. Whip the cream lightly. Place one cake on a serving plate and spread with the cream. Scatter with the fruit and cover with the remaining cake.

For the decoration, break the chocolate into pieces. Bring the cream to the boil in a small pan. Stir in the chocolate until it has melted. Transfer to a bowl and cool slightly. Beat the mixture until just peaking; then swirl over the top and sides of the cake.

Press white chocolate caraque gently over the top and sides, and dust lightly with cocoa powder. Chill until ready to serve.

*Opposite: White Chocolate Gâteau.*

*Next page: Buche de Noël.*

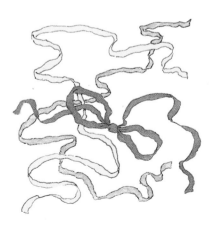

## Buche de Noël

Serves 10

3 eggs
3 oz/⅓ cup superfine sugar, plus extra for sprinkling
2 oz/½ cup all-purpose flour
2 tablespoons cocoa powder

Filling:

3 oz/3 squares milk chocolate
¼ pint/⅔ cup heavy cream
2 tablespoons brandy or rum

To Decorate:

8 oz/8 squares dark chocolate
¼ pint/⅔ cup heavy cream
1 oz/1 square white chocolate
Chocolate caraque (p.7)
Sprigs of holly
Confectioners' sugar for dusting

Grease and line a 13x9 inch jelly roll pan. Place the eggs and sugar in a large heatproof bowl, set over a saucepan of simmering water, and beat with an electric mixer until the mixture leaves a trail when the beater is lifted from the bowl. Remove from the heat and beat until cooled. Sift the flour and cocoa powder into the bowl and fold in using a large metal spoon. Turn into the prepared pan and smooth the mixture gently into the corners. Bake in a preheated oven at 400°F for 12–15 minutes until just firm to the touch.

Sprinkle a clean sheet of parchment paper with superfine sugar and invert the cake on to it. Peel away the lining paper and then roll the cake up in the clean paper. Leave to cool.

To make the filling, chop the milk chocolate finely. Beat the cream and brandy or rum until just peaking and then fold in the chocolate. Unroll the cake carefully and spread with the filling. Roll the cake up again and transfer to a cake board or plate. Cut a thick diagonal slice off one end and attach to one side.

To decorate, break the dark chocolate into pieces. Bring the cream to the boil in a small pan. Remove from the heat and stir in the chocolate until it has melted. Transfer to a bowl and leave to cool.

Beat the chocolate cream lightly until peaking and then spread all over the roulade, swirling attractively with a palette knife. Melt the white chocolate and place in a pastry bag fitted with a writing tip. Use to pile spirals at the ends of the log. Lay the chocolate caraque decoratively over the log and decorate with some sprigs of holly. Dust generously with confectioners' sugar and chill until ready to serve.

# INDEX